# Patterns

## Table of Contents

# Patterns with Colors

Circle the color based on the pattern.

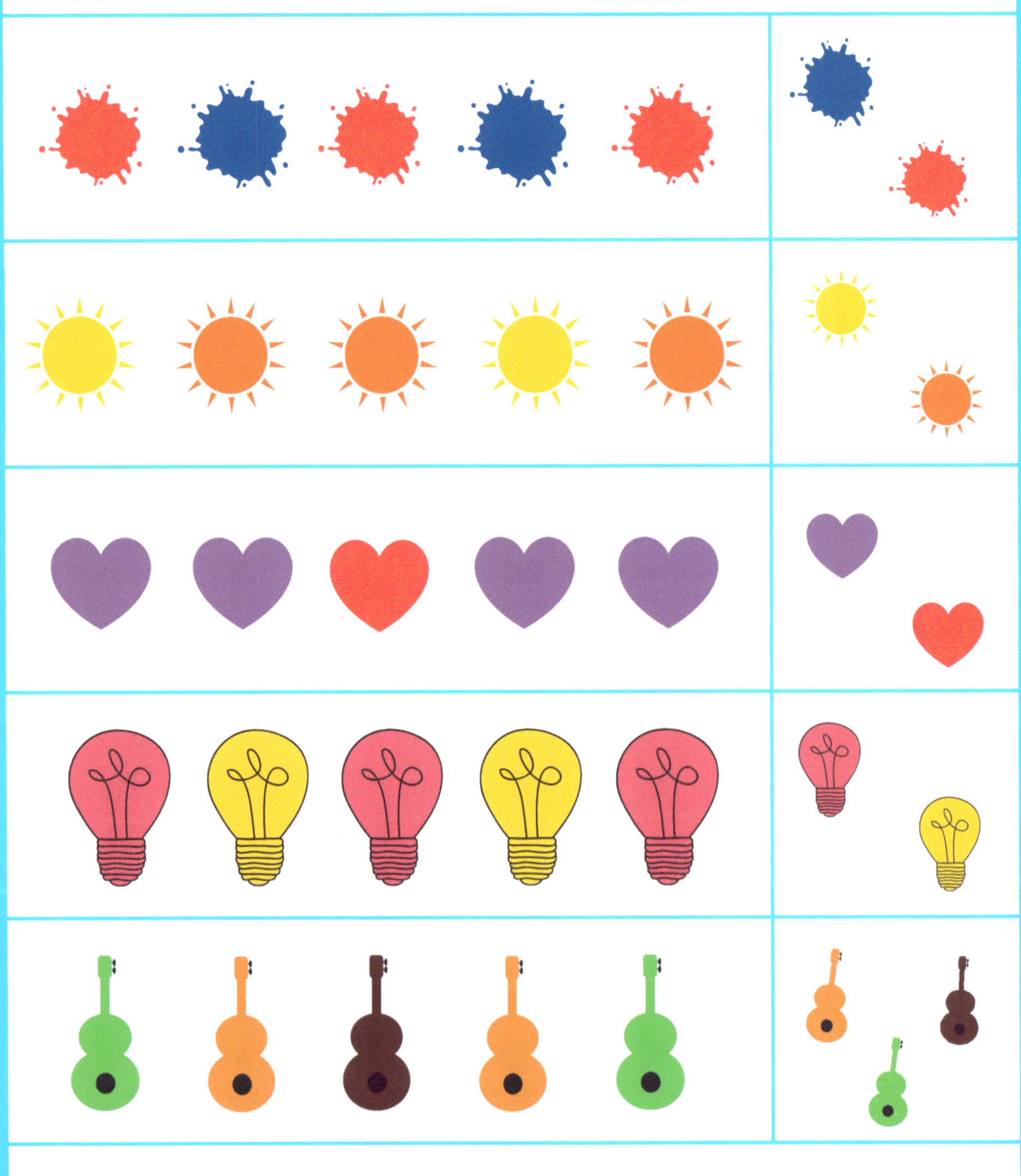

# Patterns with Colors

Circle the color based on the pattern.

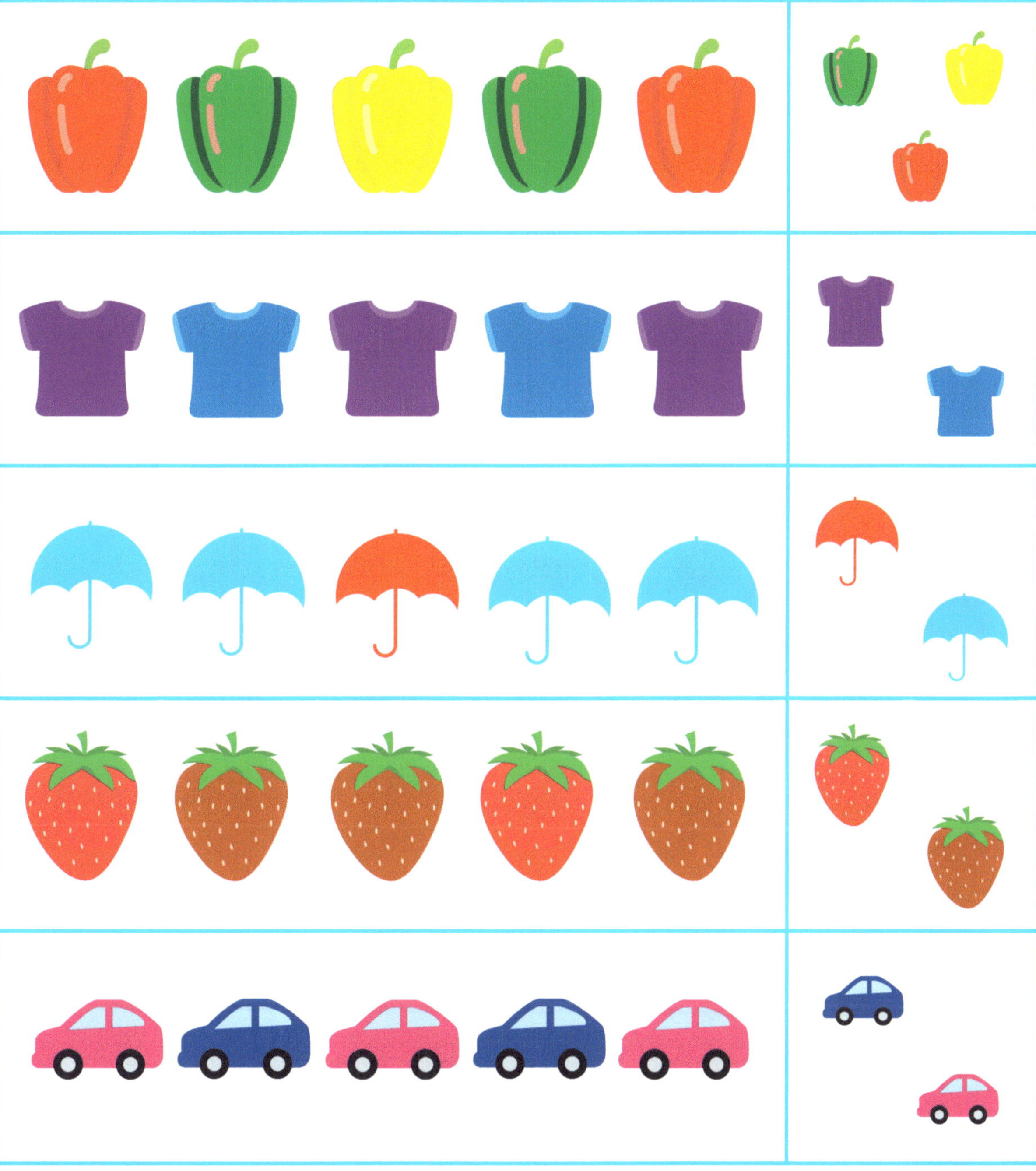

# Patterns with Colors

Circle the color based on the pattern.

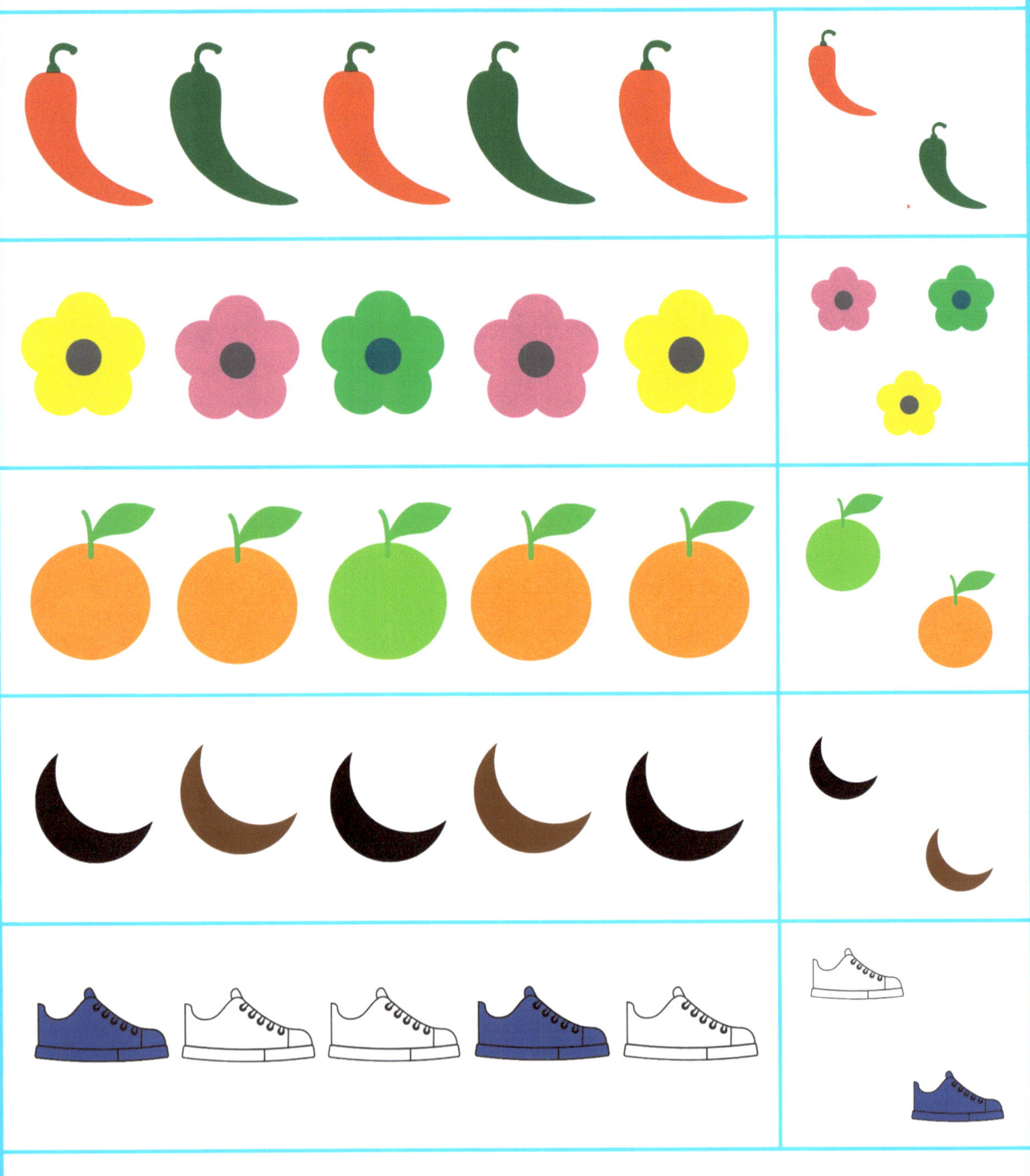

# Patterns with Colors

Cut and paste the correct color based on the pattern.

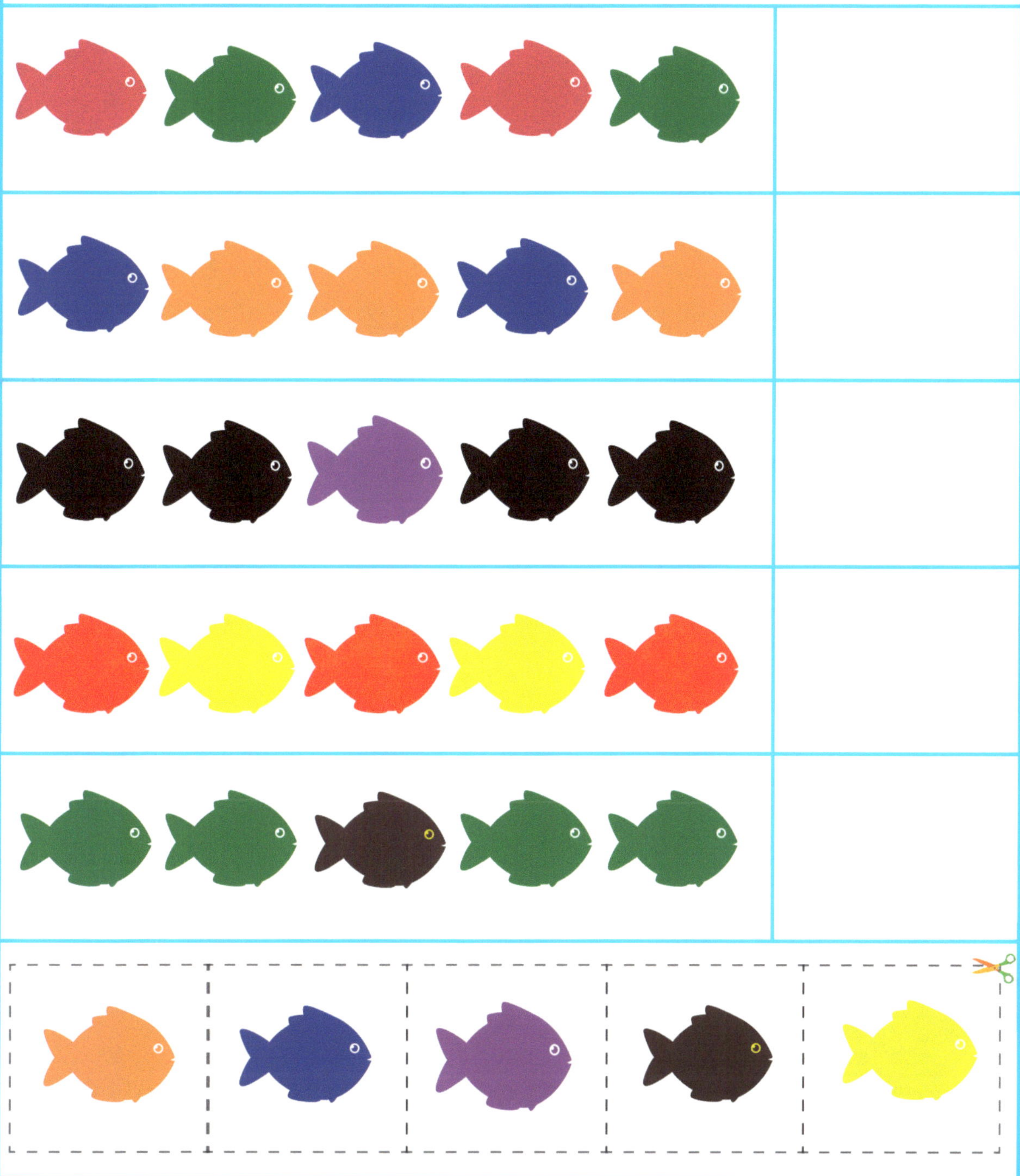

# Patterns with Colors

Cut and paste the correct color based on the pattern.

# Patterns with Colors

Color the shape in the middle based on the pattern.

# Patterns with Colors

Color the shape in the middle based on the pattern.

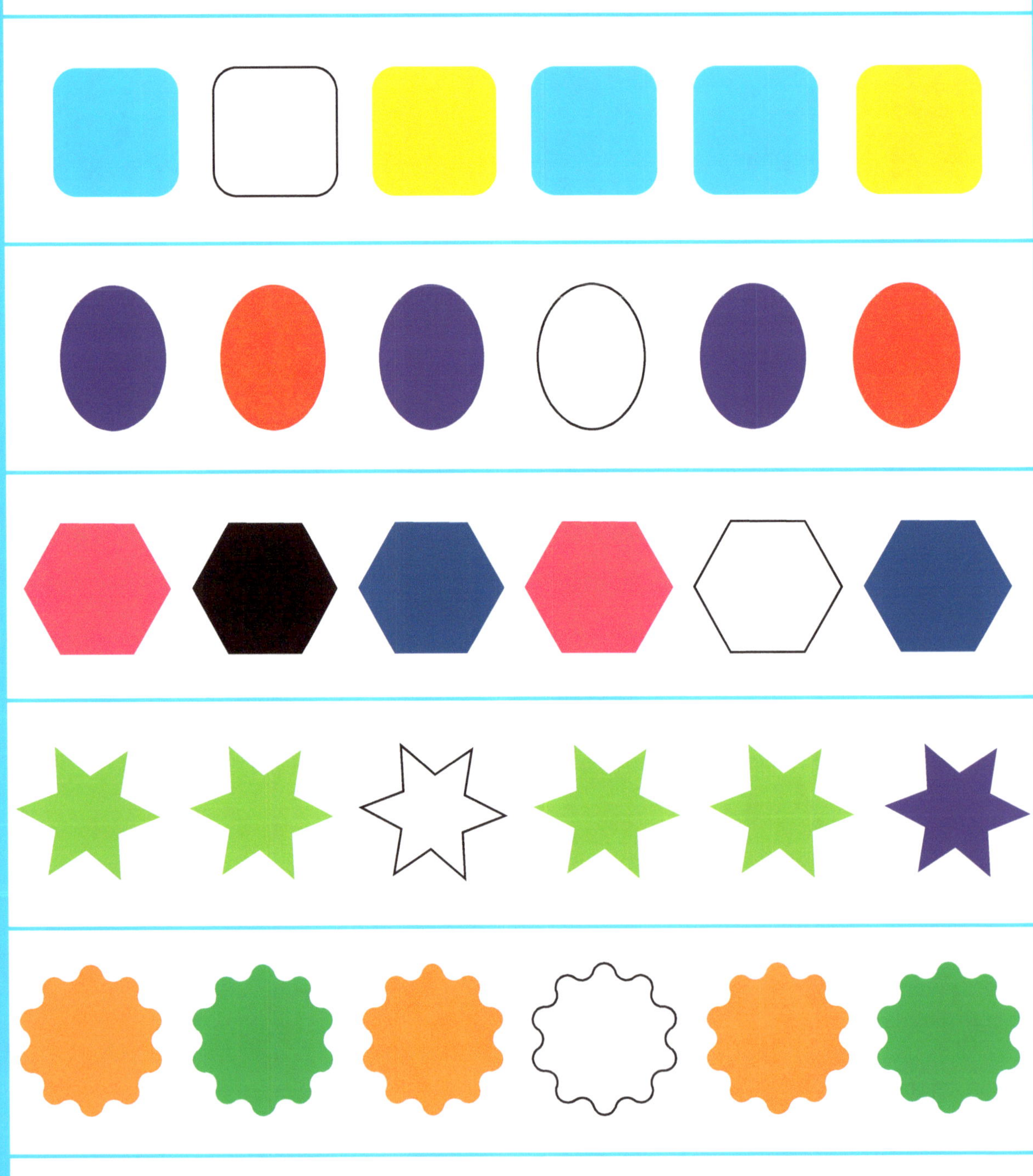

# Pattern Cards with Colors

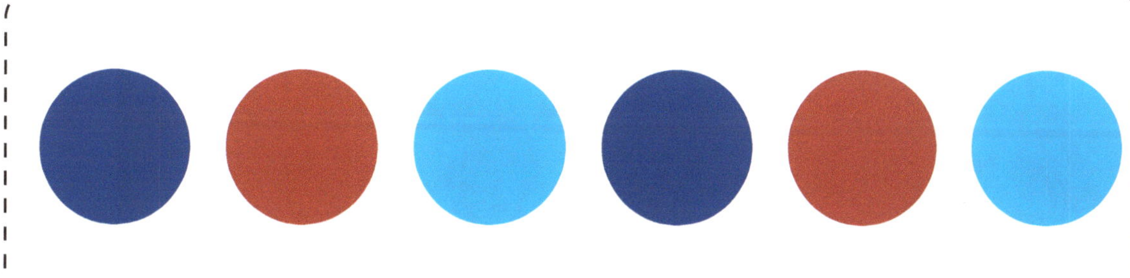

# Patterns with Shapes

Circle the shape based on the pattern.

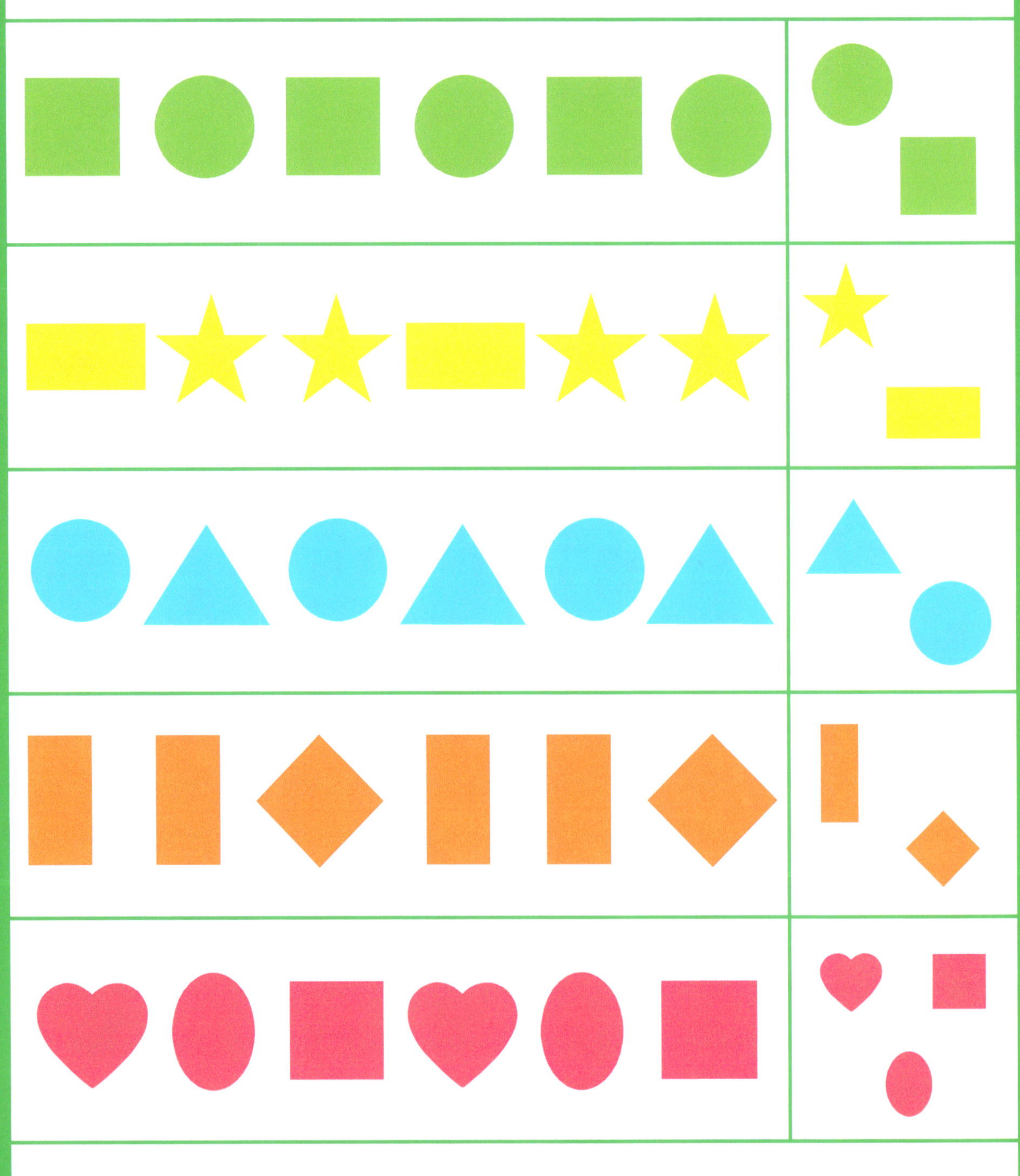

# Patterns with Shapes

Circle the shape based on the pattern.

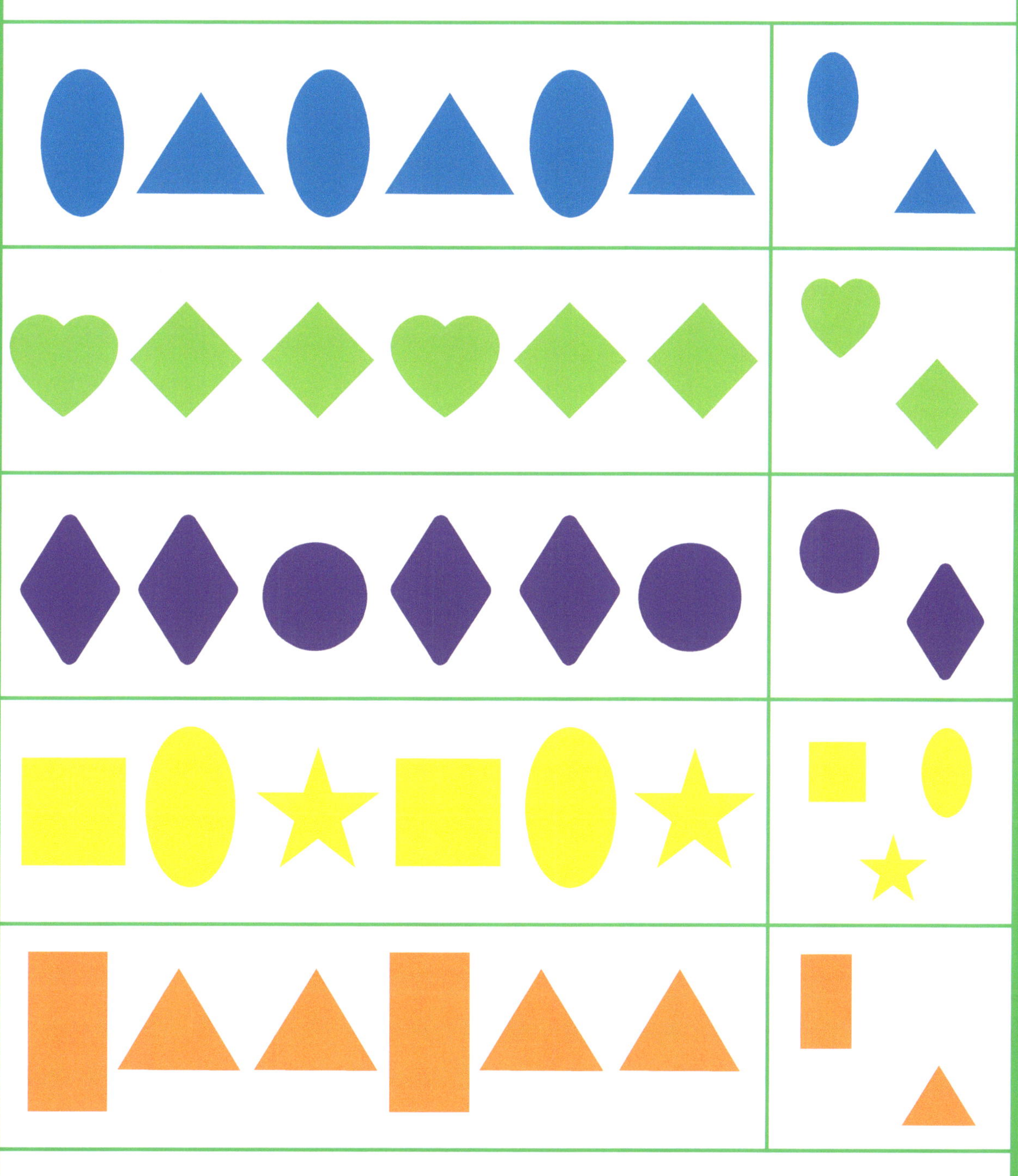

# Patterns with Shapes

Circle the shape based on the pattern.

# Patterns with Shapes

Cut and paste the correct shape based on the pattern.

# Patterns with Shapes

Cut and paste the correct shape based on the pattern.

# Patterns with Shapes

Draw the shape based on the pattern.

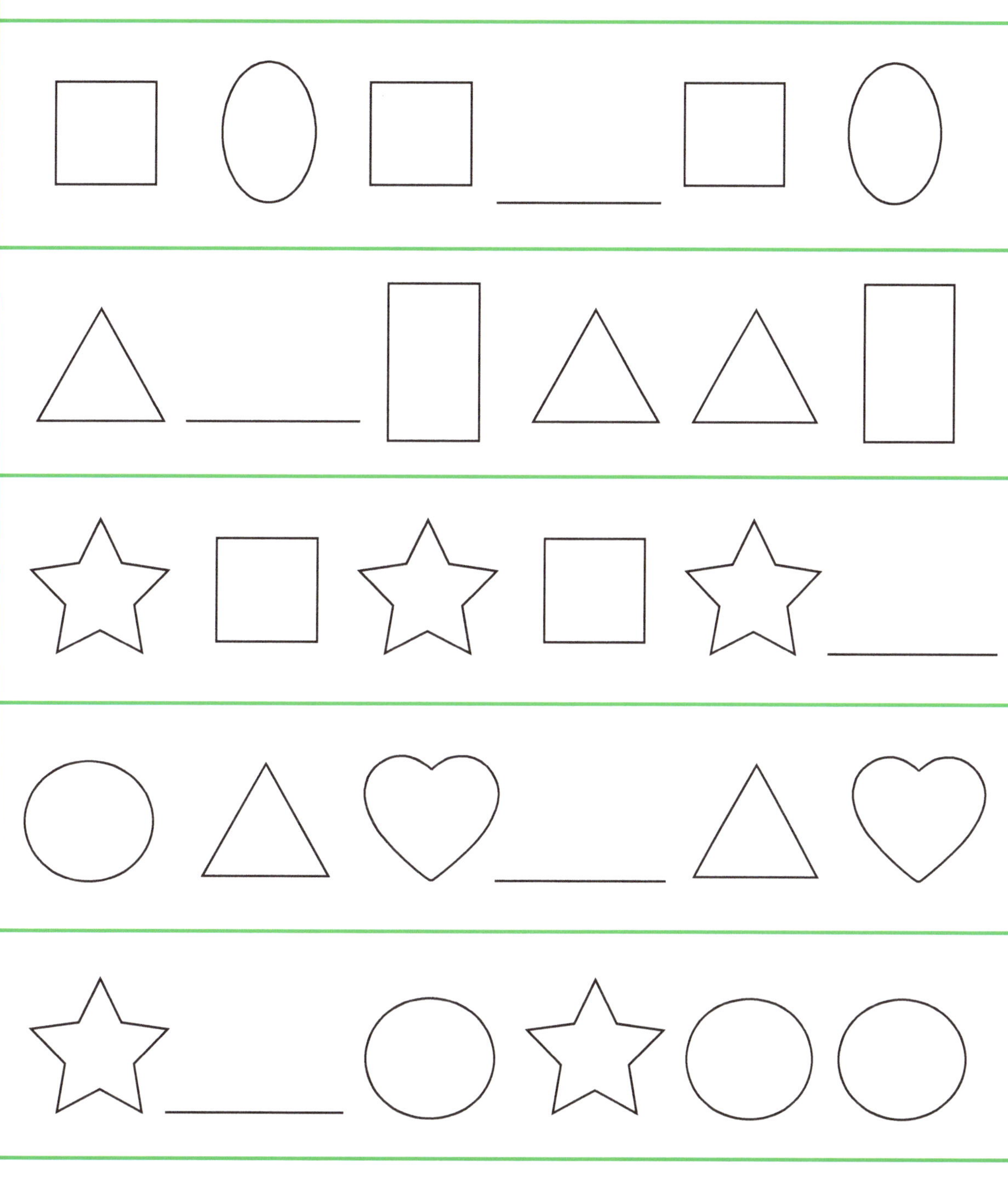

# Patterns with Shapes

Draw the shape based on the pattern.

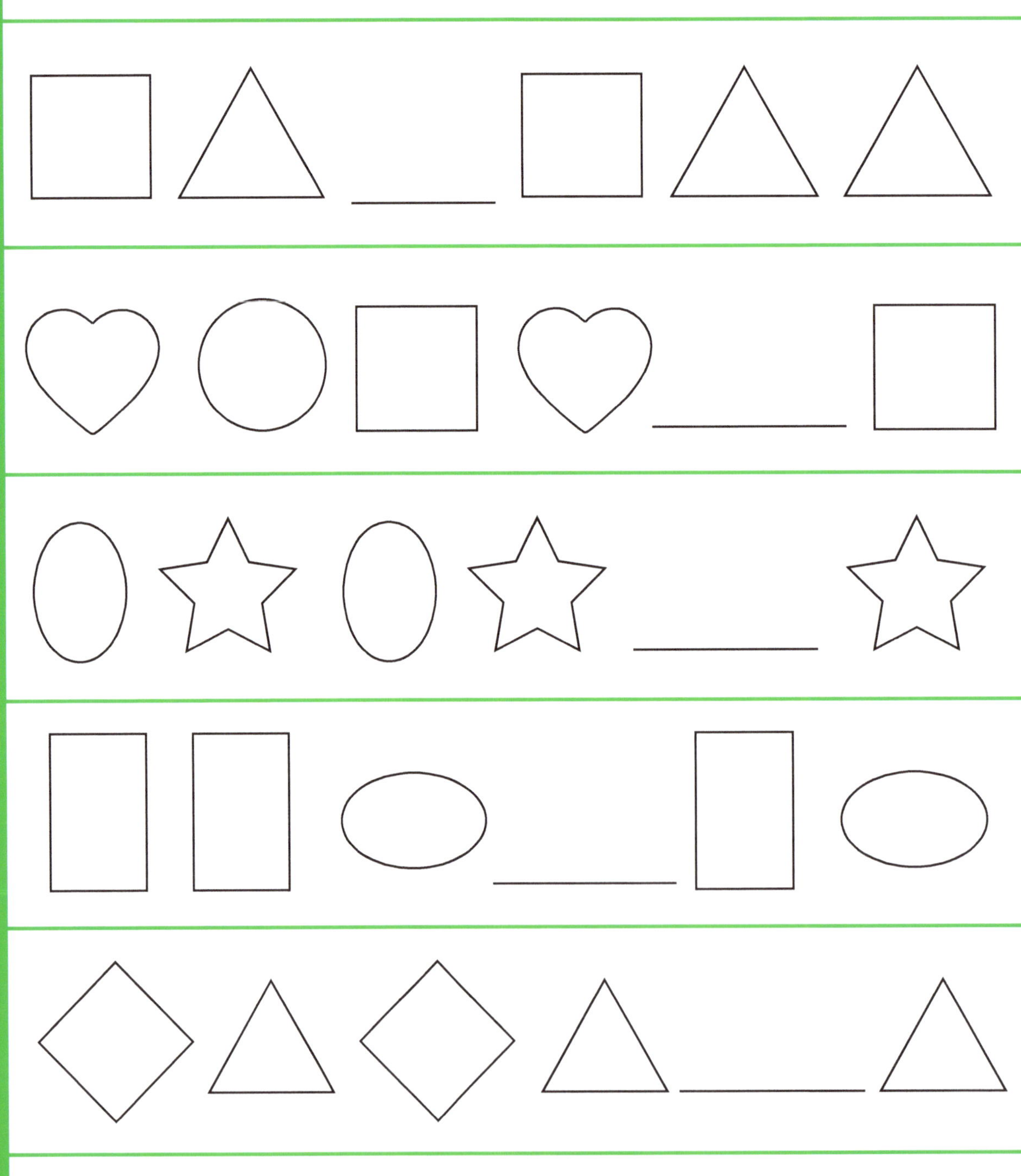

# Pattern Cards with Shapes

# Patterns with Pictures

Circle the picture based on the pattern.

# Patterns with Pictures

Circle the picture based on the pattern.

# Patterns with Pictures

Circle the picture based on the pattern.

# Patterns with Pictures

Cut and paste the correct picture based on the pattern.

# Patterns with Pictures

Cut and paste the correct picture based on the pattern.

# Patterns with Pictures

Circle the picture based on the pattern.

# Patterns with Pictures

Circle the picture based on the pattern.

# Pattern Cards with Pictures